Beyond the Players
Announcers

by Allan Morey

Bullfrog
Books

Ideas for Parents and Teachers

Bullfrog Books let children practice reading informational text at the earliest reading levels. Repetition, familiar words, and photo labels support early readers.

Before Reading

- Discuss the cover photo. What does it tell them?

- Look at the picture glossary together. Read and discuss the words.

Read the Book

- "Walk" through the book and look at the photos. Let the child ask questions. Point out the photo labels.

- Read the book to the child, or have him or her read independently.

After Reading

- Prompt the child to think more. Ask: Have you ever been to a sporting event? Did you hear an announcer?

Bullfrog Books are published by Jump!
5357 Penn Avenue South
Minneapolis, MN 55419
www.jumplibrary.com

Library of Congress Cataloging-in-Publication Data

Names: Morey, Allan, author.
Title: Announcers / Allan Morey.
Description: Minneapolis, MN: Jump!, Inc., [2024]
Series: Beyond the players | Includes index.
Audience: Ages 5–8 years
Identifiers: LCCN 2023024690 (print)
LCCN 2023024691 (ebook)
ISBN 9798889966418 (hardcover)
ISBN 9798889966425 (paperback)
ISBN 9798889966432 (ebook)
Subjects: LCSH: Mass media and sports—Juvenile literature. | Sportscasters—Juvenile literature. Television broadcasting of sports—Juvenile literature. Radio broadcasting of sports—Juvenile literature.
Classification: LCC GV742 .M67 2024 (print)
LCC GV742 (ebook)
DDC 796.092—dc23/eng/20230627
LC record available at https://lccn.loc.gov/2023024690
LC ebook record available at https://lccn.loc.gov/2023024691

Editor: Jenna Gleisner
Designer: Emma Almgren-Bersie

Photo Credits: Rich von Biberstein/Icon Sportswire/AP Images, cover; SDI Productions/iStock, 1; Marcel Paschertz/Shutterstock, 3; Dmytro Aksonov/iStock, 4; Stu Forster/Getty, 5; Leonard Zhukovsky/Shutterstock, 6–7, 10, 23bl; Gail Burton/AP Images, 8–9, 23tl; Bobkov Evgeniy/Shutterstock, 11 (foreground), 23br; vm/iStock, 11 (background), 23tr; Steve Jacobson/Shutterstock, 12–13, 22tr; Marco Ciccolella/Shutterstock, 14–15; Eakin Howard/Getty, 16–17; Natursports/Shutterstock, 18; Sportimage Ltd/Alamy, 19, 23tm; Mordolff/iStock, 20–21; PA Images/Alamy, 22tl; Keeton Gale/Shutterstock, 22bl; gorodenkoff/iStock, 22br; AlexLMX/Shutterstock, 23bm; Photoongraphy/Shutterstock, 24.

Printed in the United States of America at Corporate Graphics in North Mankato, Minnesota.

Table of Contents

Who Scored?... 4

On the Job... 22

Picture Glossary... 23

Index 24

To Learn More... 24

Who Scored?

We are at a soccer game.

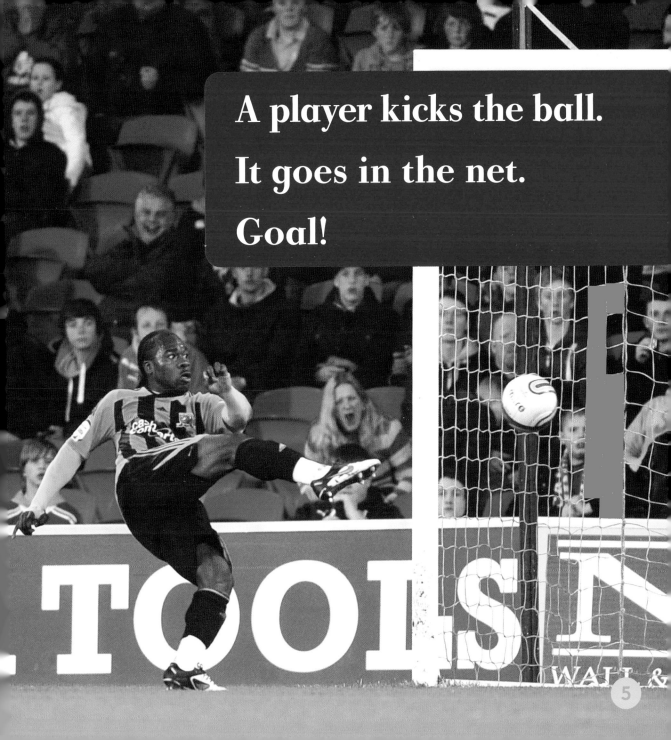

A player kicks the ball.

It goes in the net.

Goal!

Who tells us the score?

Announcers!

They sit in the media box.

announcers

media
box

7

They watch the game.

They say what happens.

How do we hear them?
They talk into microphones.

microphone

speaker

Speakers play the sound.

A player catches the ball!
Announcers say who.
They help fans follow
the game.

puck

A player has the puck.
Who has it?
They tell us.

A player hits the ball.

Where?

They tell us.

Score!

They announce it.

They cheer, too.
Yay!

Do you love sports?

Do you want to announce?

You can!

On the Job

Announcers tell fans what happens during a sporting event. What do they announce? Take a look!

cheer
Announcers are fans, too! They celebrate and cheer.

play-by-play action
Announcers tell fans what is happening during a game.

players
Announcers tell fans about players.

score
Announcers tell fans the score.

BEYOND THE PLAYERS

ANNOUNCERS

Bullfrog Books

Picture Glossary

announce
To say something officially.

cheer
To praise or encourage with shouts.

fans
People who are very interested in or enthusiastic about something.

media box
A special section of a stadium or arena where members of the media sit.

microphones
Devices that make sounds louder.

speakers
Machines that make sounds loud enough to be heard in a large area.

Index

announce 18, 21

cheer 19

fans 12

game 4, 9, 12

goal 5

media box 6

microphones 10

player 5, 12, 15, 16

score 6, 18

speakers 11

tells 6, 15, 16

watch 9

To Learn More

FACT SURFER

Finding more information is as easy as 1, 2, 3.

① Go to www.factsurfer.com

② Enter "announcers" into the search box.

③ Choose your book to see a list of websites.